Terry Jennings

Electricity and Magnetism

Contents

Cover photograph:

*Electrical energy is
supplied to the
National Grid from the
coal-fired power station
at Didcot, England.*

Coordinating author:

Terry Jennings

Language consultant:

Diana Bentley

Additional contributions:

Nick Axten, Claire Axten

Note: Some spreads have been specially prepared for easier access.
These are identified in **bold** print in the Contents' list above.

What magnets do

Have you ever played with a magnet? If you have, you probably know that a magnet will pick up some things. It picks up certain metal objects. But it doesn't pick up all metal things. And it doesn't pick up anything not made of metal.

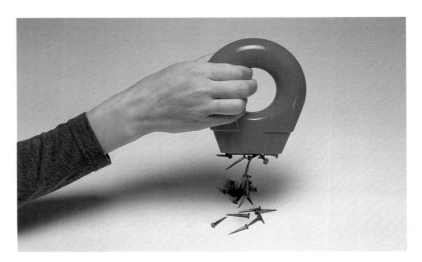

A magnet will only pick up some metal objects.

We often use magnets for holding things.

Magnets large and small

Most magnets are manufactured. They have been made by people. Nearly all are made from iron or steel. Magnets are of all shapes and sizes and strengths.

Some magnets are not very strong, like those used to fix notices to metal boards. Small magnets also hold the doors of refrigerators and wardrobes shut.

There are lots of other magnets, often much stronger, that you cannot usually see. Washing machines, radios, and vacuum cleaners all need magnets to work. Telephones and television sets contain magnets, and so do computers and tape-recorders. Electric motors contain magnets.

Magnets are also used in power stations to produce the electricity we use every day in our homes and schools.

Electromagnets

Some magnets use electricity and can be switched on and off. These are called **electromagnets**. When electricity flows through them, they act as magnets. Very large electromagnets are used to sort metals. Electromagnets are used to pick up old cars and other huge pieces of scrap iron or steel.

🍎 **The world's largest electromagnet is at a research station near Moscow. It is 60 m in diameter and weighs 36,000 tonnes.**

Lodestone is a natural magnet

Natural magnets

In some places magnets are found in the ground. These are **natural magnets**, and they are called **lodestones**. Lodestones are made of a black rock called **magnetite**. Magnetite contains iron. Long ago, people knew that a piece of lodestone would pick up small pieces of iron.

🍎 **Focus**   natural magnet   lodestone   magnetite   electromagnet

Making magnets

One way to make a magnet is to use a piece of steel. A large sewing needle or a steel knitting-needle will do. Stroke the needle with the end of a magnet lots of times – try 20 times to start with. You must always stroke the needle with the same end of the magnet and in the same direction. Turning a piece of magnetic material into a magnet is called **magnetizing**.

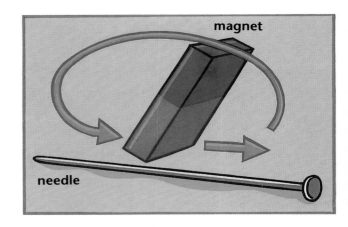

How a magnet works

A piece of magnetic material, such as iron or steel, consists of millions of tiny magnets. When these tiny magnets all face in different directions and pull in different directions, they cancel each other out. The little magnets do *not* add up to make one big magnet.

When you stroke a piece of magnetic material, such as steel with a magnet, you make all the tiny magnets begin to turn in the same direction. The more you stroke the piece of steel, the more the little magnets get into line and the stronger the new magnet becomes.

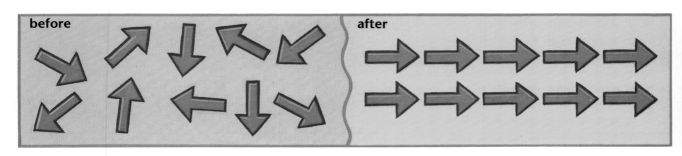

What happens when a piece of iron is magnetized

Taking care of magnets

A magnet you have made, or one you have bought, will stay a magnet as long as you use it carefully. If you drop a magnet or hit it hard, it will be weakened slightly. Some of the tiny magnets will move out of line. All magnets can be weakened if you drop them or hit them hard. They can also be weakened if you heat them.

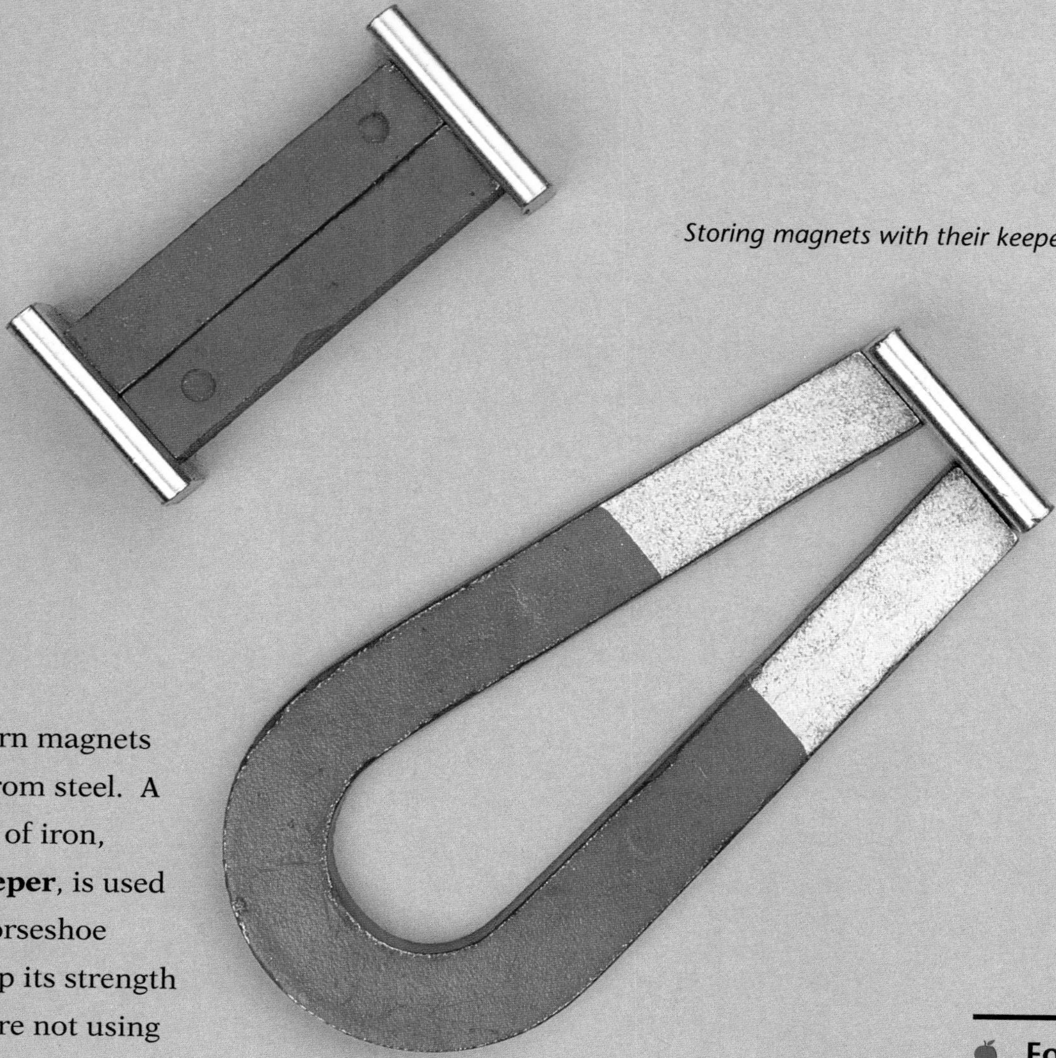

Storing magnets with their keepers

Most modern magnets are made from steel. A small piece of iron, called a **keeper**, is used to help a horseshoe magnet keep its strength when you are not using it. Bar magnets are stored in pairs. A keeper is placed at each end of the pair.

🍎 **Focus**

magnetize

keeper

5

The Earth is a magnet

The Earth we live on is magnetic. It behaves as if it had a giant magnet inside it. One end of this magnet is called the **north magnetic pole**. The other end is the **south magnetic pole**. Magnets are affected by the Earth's giant magnet.

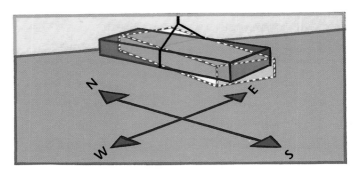

A bar magnet will swing round until one end points North.

The compass

Nearly a thousand years ago, sailors and other travellers first hung pieces of lodestone from a thread to make **compasses**. Today people still use magnetic compasses to help them find the way. Ships, aircraft, and explorers use compasses.

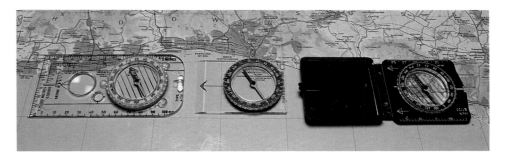

The needle of a compass is a thin magnet.

The box of the compass has to be made of a non-magnetic material such as brass, wood or plastic. If the box were made of a magnetic metal, such as iron or steel, the needle would be attracted to the box and not show the right direction. Compasses in ships and aircraft are usually filled with a liquid. This stops the needle from swinging round too wildly.

The Earth's magnetism

The north and south magnetic poles of the Earth do not lie right underneath the geographical North and South Poles. (The geographical North and South Poles are the points around which the Earth rotates.) At present the north magnetic pole is in Canada, about 2,000 kilometres away from the geographic North Pole. But the magnetic poles move slowly. The end of a compass that points towards the north magnetic pole is called a **North-seeking pole**. The end that points towards the south magnetic pole is called a **South-seeking pole**.

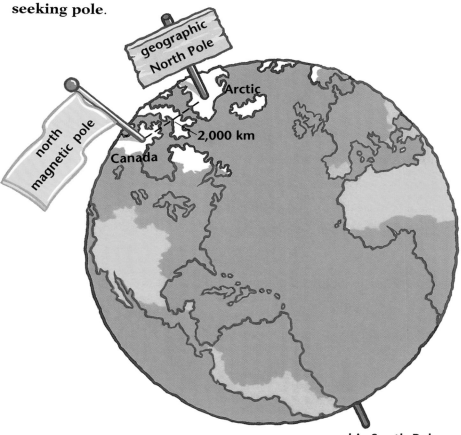

geographic North Pole

Arctic

2,000 km

Canada

north magnetic pole

geographic South Pole

● **Pigeons, salmon, bees, and some other animals have tiny magnets inside their bodies. Scientists think these animals are able to use the Earth's magnetism to help them find their way.**

● Focus

north magnetic pole
south magnetic pole
compass
North-seeking pole
South-seeking pole

Magnetic fields (1)

A magnet pulls or attracts certain materials to it. This force of attraction is called magnetism. A material that can be attracted by a magnet is called magnetic.

There are different kinds of magnetic materials. The most common is iron. All objects made of iron are magnetic. The metals cobalt and nickel and most kinds of steel are magnetic.

A magnet can be used to separate steel cans from aluminium ones.

 Tin is not magnetic. Magnets attract 'tin cans' because the cans are mainly steel. They have only a thin coating of tin to help stop the can from rusting.

Magnetic poles

The pull, or attraction, of a magnet is strongest at its ends. These are called the magnet's **poles**. If you place the North-seeking pole of one magnet near the South-seeking pole of another, they will attract each other. But if you place the North-seeking pole near the North-seeking pole of the second magnet, they will push each other away. We say the two poles repel each other.

In the same way, two South-seeking poles will repel each other. You may find it easy to remember that:

'Like poles repel, unlike poles attract'.

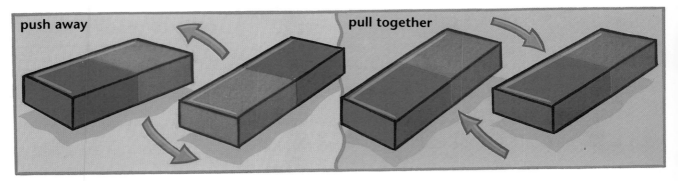

push away   pull together

Like poles of magnets repel each other.   *Unlike poles of magnets attract each other.*

High-speed trains

The force of repulsion can be used for very practical ideas. Some high-speed trains, called Maglev trains, use the force of strong magnets repelling each other. Both the train and the track contain powerful electromagnets. The magnets are arranged so that the poles of the track magnets face the same poles of the train magnets. The poles repel each other and the train hovers over the track.

🍎 **Repulsion is the only true test for magnetism as only two magnets will repel one another.**

Magnetic fields

Although the magnetic force is strongest at the poles of a magnet, it can be felt some way away from the magnet. If a magnet is covered with a thin sheet of paper and iron filings are scattered over the sheet, the iron filings form a pattern. This pattern is called the **magnetic field** of the magnet. Inside the field of a magnet the forces of attraction and repulsion are 'felt' by magnetic materials. A magnetic field can pass through materials like air, water, paper, and glass.

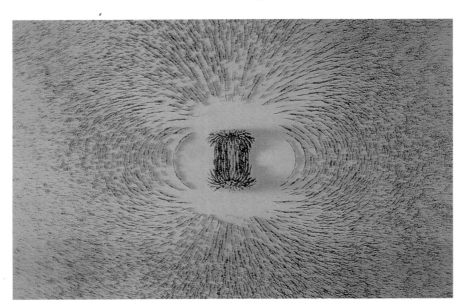

The pattern of the magnetic field of a bar magnet.

🍎 **Focus**

pole

magnetic field

9

Magnetic Fields (2)

Materials that are **non-magnetic**, like air, water, plastic, wood, glass, paper, and cardboard, let the force of magnetism pass through them. Because it passes through such materials, magnetism can be a nuisance. For example, many watches have cases made of plastic, but inside parts are made of steel. If you put a strong magnet near a watch, the magnetism can affect the parts inside. It may slow down the working of the watch and even stop it altogether.

All these have magnetic coatings on which 'information' is stored.

A magnet can also damage a tape-recorder, video-recorder or computer. The magnetism of even a small magnet can sometimes pass right through the case of one of these machines and stop it working properly.

Tape-recorders and video-recorders work by changing sound waves or pictures into magnetism. The recording tape is plastic with a metal coating. At each point along the tape the metal is magnetized. The strength and direction of the magnetism change along the tape. The sound or pictures are recorded as this magnetic pattern. When the tape is played, the magnetic pattern is turned back into sounds or pictures are produced according to the **information** in the magnetic pattern. Similarly the programs and data of a computer are stored on magnetic discs or tapes. If you bring a magnet too near recording tapes or computer discs, it can alter their magnetism, so that all the information they contained is lost for ever.

Inside a television set

Inside a television set, beams of tiny particles (called **electrons**) are fired at the screen from an *electron gun*. When the beams strike the back of the screen, they produce dots of light that make up the picture. Magnetic coils make the beams move across the screen.

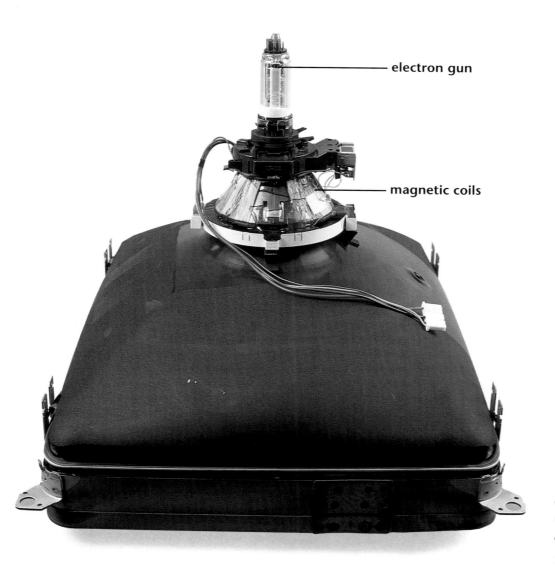

electron gun

magnetic coils

A television set uses magnetic coils to help produce the picture.

Switching magnetism on and off

An **electromagnet** is a piece of iron with a coil of plastic-covered wire round it. When electricity passes through the wire, the iron becomes a magnet. When the electricity is switched off, the iron stops being a magnet. It is a **temporary magnet**.

Steel can be used in an electromagnet instead of iron. However, the steel keeps its magnetism when the electricity is turned off. That is how most **permanent magnets** are made.

This electromagnetic crane is used for sorting scrap metals.

Using electromagnets

Electromagnets are used in scrap-yards for separating iron and steel from other metals. An electromagnetic crane will pick up iron and steel when the electricity is switched on. The other metals are not picked up. When the electricity is switched off, the crane drops the iron and steel.

Powerful electromagnets are found in hospitals. They are used to remove iron or steel splinters from eyes. Electric bells, telephones, the loudspeakers in television sets, and stereo equipment also use electromagnets.

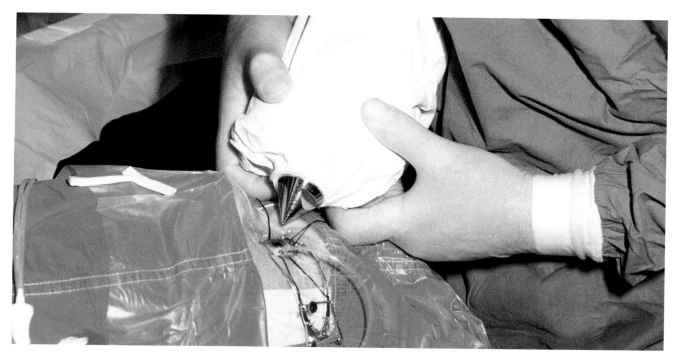

Using an electromagnet to remove a steel splinter from a patient's eye.

A home-made electromagnet

You can easily make a small electromagnet from a length of covered wire and a large iron nail. The wire is wrapped around the nail and the ends connected to a small battery. (The battery will not last long if used in this way and the coil may become quite hot.)

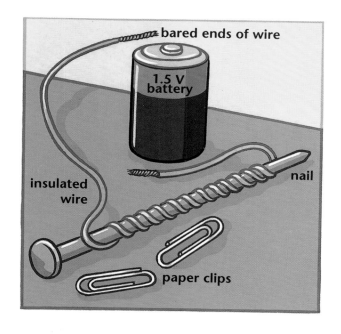

bared ends of wire

1.5 V battery

insulated wire

nail

paper clips

Focus   electromagnet   temporary magnet   permanent magnet

Using electricity

Electricity makes electromagnets work. And magnets can be used to make electricity. Electricity is a form of **energy** we use every day. In homes and schools electricity is turned into other forms of energy. Electrical energy becomes **heat** energy for cooking food or warming rooms. Electric fires, ovens, irons, and kettles use electricity. Electrical energy is turned into **light** energy in lamps and torches, or into **sound** energy in door-bells, telephones, and burglar alarms. Washing machines, dishwashers, and food-mixers turn electrical energy into **movement** energy. Electricity drives the motor in a vacuum cleaner sucking up dust and dirt from floors and carpets. Electricity keeps our food cool so that it doesn't go bad - refrigerators and freezers use electricity.

How many objects can you see which use electricity?

Electricity outdoors

Outside our homes, electricity works many kinds of lights and signs. It powers many trains and even a few cars, vans, and buses. How many other uses of electricity can you think of?

How is electricity being used here?

Using electricity safely

We use electricity so much because it is an easy-to-use form of energy. Electricity is very easy to control, and very quick - it is there at the flick of a switch.

But electricity has many **dangers**. It is safe to experiment with torch batteries as long as you use them in the normal way. But you must not damage them or try to connect them to the mains.

 You should never interfere with electricity from the mains in any way. It could burn you badly, or even kill you.

 Focus electricity   energy   heat   light   sound   movement   danger

15

Making a path for electricity

You do not always use electricity from the mains in your home. Quite often you will use a battery. Torches, radios, calculators, watches, and cameras are worked by batteries.

A circuit is a loop

If you connect a bulb and a battery in the right way, the bulb lights up. When you do this, you have made an electrical **circuit**. The circuit is a loop, running from one of the battery's connectors, or terminals, through the bulb to the other terminal, then through the battery and out of the first terminal. It has no beginning and no end. The circuit is the path along which the electricity moves. Every circuit has to be a loop.

Electricity flows around the whole circuit. It flows through the wires, the bulb and the battery. You cannot see the electricity in a circuit like this. You can only see what it does. When electricity flows it makes the bulb light. The battery is needed to make electricity flow. It pushes the electricity around the circuit.

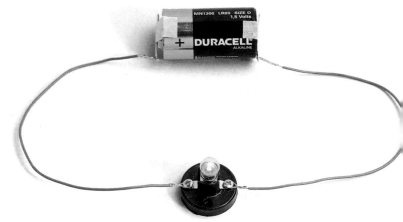

A simple circuit

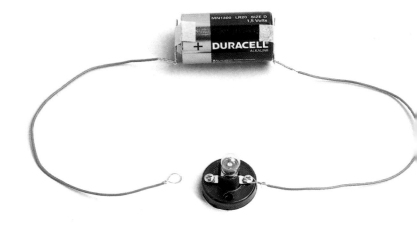

The bulb in this picture doesn't light. Can you see why? What would you do to make it light?

Opening and closing a circuit

A **closed circuit** is one that has no opening, or gap in it. As long as there is a gap it is an **open circuit**. Electricity cannot flow across the gap, so the bulb does not light.

In order to turn an electric light on or off, you generally use a **switch**. Have you ever wondered how a switch works? It is a way of closing or opening a gap in an electrical circuit. Using a switch is easier than touching two wires together. It is also safer.

In an electric light circuit, you may fix a switch on either side of the bulb. Electricity that flows through the bulb and the switch must also flow through the switch. Electricity flows through the bulb only when the switch is 'on' so that the gap in the circuit is closed. When the switch is 'off', the gap is open and electricity cannot flow.

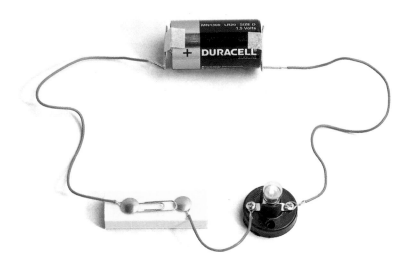

A simple circuit with the switch turned 'on'

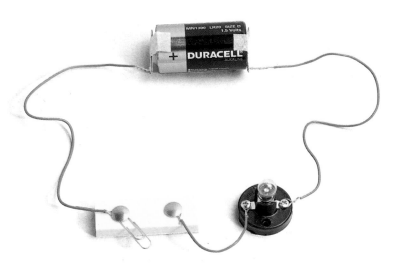

A simple circuit with the switch turned 'off'

🍎 **Electricity in movement is called electric current. Current is measured in *amps* named after the French scientist André Ampère, who died in 1836.**

🍎 **Focus**   circuit   closed circuit   open circuit   switch

Series and parallel

Did you know that you can light several bulbs with one battery? The picture shows one way of doing this. Here the electricity from the battery flows through each one of the bulbs in turn. These bulbs are connected **in series**.

The bulbs are not very bright. This is because less electricity comes from the battery when there are several bulbs in series than when there is only one. If one bulb is unscrewed, all the bulbs go out because there is now a gap in the circuit. Many Christmas tree lights have a **series circuit** like this. If one bulb breaks, all the lights go out.

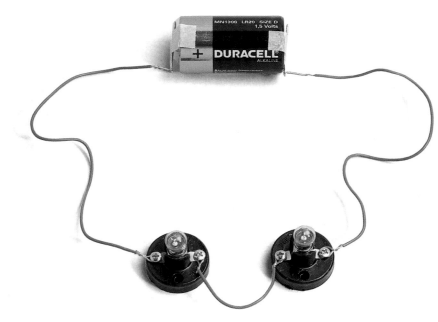

A circuit with two bulbs in series

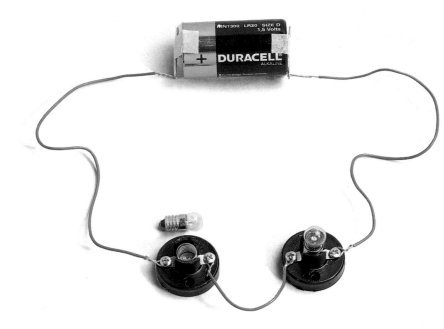

In a series circuit, unscrewing one bulb makes the others go out.

A parallel circuit

There is another way of lighting several bulbs with one battery. In this kind of circuit, some electricity flows through each bulb. These bulbs are connected **in parallel**.

Bulbs are brighter when they are connected in parallel than when they are connected in series. And if you unscrew one bulb, the others will stay alight. That is because each one has its own separate circuit to the battery. The electric lights in your home or school are connected in a **parallel circuit** like this.

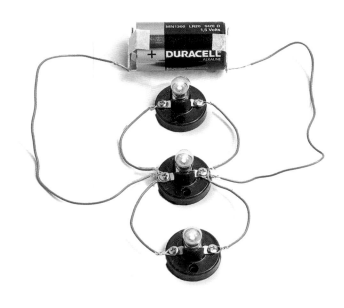

A circuit with three bulbs in parallel

Part of the parallel circuit in a house

🍎 **Batteries run out much more quickly when bulbs are connected in parallel.**

🍎 **Focus**   in series   series circuit   in parallel   parallel circuit

Joining forces

Often several batteries are used in a circuit. Like bulbs, batteries may be connected in different ways.

Joining batteries in parallel

One way to connect batteries is so that the tops of all of them are joined together. All the bottoms of the batteries are connected together. The batteries are said to be connected **in parallel.**

A bulb connected to batteries in a parallel circuit does not give a brighter light than it would if it were connected to just one battery. With three batteries, the bulb will simply go on giving light for about three times as long.

Three batteries connected in parallel

Two batteries in parallel: the brightness is the same

Joining batteries in series

Batteries are usually connected **in series**. A wire connects the bottom of one battery to the top of the next battery. For each battery that you add to a series connection, the bulb will shine more brightly.

Bulbs are made for a certain number of batteries. If they are connected in series to more batteries, they 'burn out'. If they are connected to too few batteries, the bulbs give only a dim light.

Often batteries are not connected by wires. They simply touch each other, top to bottom. This is how the batteries in many torches are arranged.

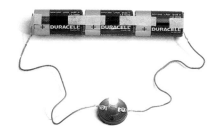

Too much electricity is flowing here.

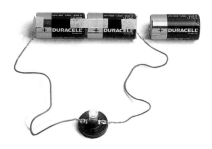

Just the right amount of electricity

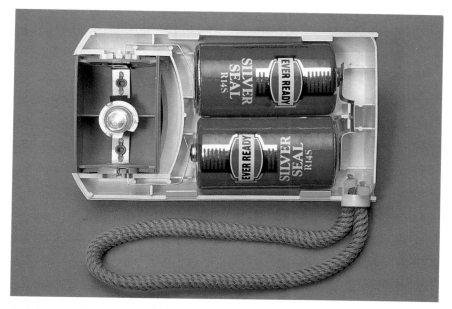

Too little electricity for this bulb

Inside a torch. Can you follow the path of the electricity from the battery, through the bulb, and back to the battery?.

🍎 **The world's largest battery is at a power-station in California, USA.**

🍎 **Focus**

in parallel

in series

21

Cells and batteries

A battery uses chemicals to produce electricity. The battery turns **chemical energy** into **electrical energy**. There are two types of battery. There are batteries that make electricity until all their chemicals are used up. Then they are thrown away. A torch battery is like this. Another type of battery is called a **rechargeable** battery. When the electricity in this type of battery is used up, you can put more into it - you recharge the battery. A car has a battery like this.

🍎 **WARNING Never touch a car battery.**

Electric cells

The proper name for a single battery like the one shown in the picture is an electric **cell**. Inside a cell like this is a damp chemical paste. It is contained in a case made of a grey metal zinc. Down the centre of the cell is a rod made of a black substance, carbon. This carbon rod has a metal tip so that it makes a better connection.

Never cut open a cell or battery to look inside

When the cell is joined up in a circuit, and the switch is on, the chemicals in the paste produce an electric current. When the chemicals are used up the cell must be disposed of.

🍎 **The electric eel lives in South American rivers. It has special muscles in its body that work like batteries to produce electricity. The eel can stun its prey with a powerful electric shock.**

Inside a torch cell

Batteries

The word **battery** really means two or more cells joined together. A cell provides an electrical force that pushes electricity around the circuit. The strength of this electrical force is measured in units called **volts**. Most torch cells produce an electrical force of one-and-a-half volts. If a number of cells are joined together in series, they make a battery. Two cells joined in a battery produce three volts, and a nine-volt battery consists of six cells joined together. When the chemicals are used up the battery must be disposed of.

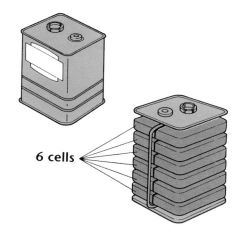

6 cells

Inside a battery

Rechargeable batteries

The most common kind of rechargeable battery is found in a car. When the car is moving, some of the energy given out by the burning fuel is turned into electricity for the lights, instruments, and so on. But the car needs electricity to work the starter motor or the lights when the car is not moving.

A car battery has to be charged up before it can be used. A car battery is always being recharged when the car's engine is running.

Most car batteries contain plates of the metal lead. These are arranged in pairs. The plates stand in sulphuric acid. Each pair of plates can give an electrical force of two volts. The whole battery gives an electrical force of 12 volts. Rechargeable batteries are also used to drive electric vehicles such as milk floats and battery-powered cars.

Inside a rechargeable battery

🍎 **Focus**   chemical energy   electrical energy   rechargeable   cell   battery

Making electricity with magnetism

Batteries and cells are very useful for making small amounts of electricity. But they do not last long and they are quite expensive. Most of the electricity we use is not made with the help of chemicals. It is made using magnetism.

The first person to make, or **generate**, electricity using magnets was the English scientist Michael Faraday in 1831. He moved an electromagnet (2) in and out of a **coil** of wire (1). This made an electric current flow through the wire. Today most of the electricity we use results from this very important discovery.

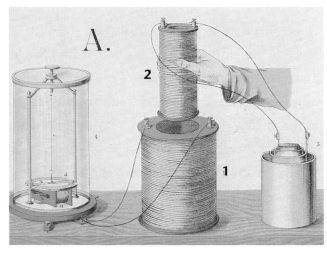

How Faraday made electricity using magnetism

A cycle dynamo

On some bicycles the lights are powered by a simple generator called a **dynamo**. The dynamo contains a magnet and a coil of wire. The magnet is shaped like a cylinder and when the bicycle wheel turns, it turns the magnet inside the coil of wire. This makes electricity flow in the wire, and the lights come on. If the bicycle stops, the dynamo stops turning and the lights go out.

A cycle dynamo

Inside a power station

Most of the electricity used in homes, schools, shops, and factories is made in a **power station**. In a power station are huge **generators**. In each generator a ring of coils of copper wire is fitted around an enormous magnet. The magnet is turned very fast and produces electricity.

Inside a power station generator hall

🍎 **When popular television programmes finish, engineers have to start extra generators working. The demand for electricity can rise by 10 per cent or more as thousands of people start to make hot drinks.**

🍎 **Focus**   generate   coil   dynamo   power station   generator

Inside a power station

Power stations still use Faraday's method to generate electricity. Faraday moved the magnet by hand. This produced only a small amount of electricity because the magnet moved slowly.

Most power stations burn a **fuel** such as coal, oil or gas to produce heat. This heat is used to boil water, turning it into steam. The steam rushes through pipes to a large wheel with blades, like a propeller, called a **turbine**. The steam flows past the blades and makes the turbine spin, up to 3,000 times every minute. The turbine is connected by a shaft to a **generator**. As the turbine turns, so does the generator which produces the electricity.

From the turbines the steam is piped to giant **cooling towers**, where it turns back into water. The hot water returns to the boiler, where it is used again, so saving both fuel and water.

Because it is difficult to store electricity, large quantities of it must be made as it is needed. In cold weather and at busy times of the day most power stations have lots of turbines and generators working to produce electricity.

A modern gas-fired power station

 Coal, oil, and gas could run out within 100 years or so. Before that happens we must find other ways to produce large quantities of electricity.

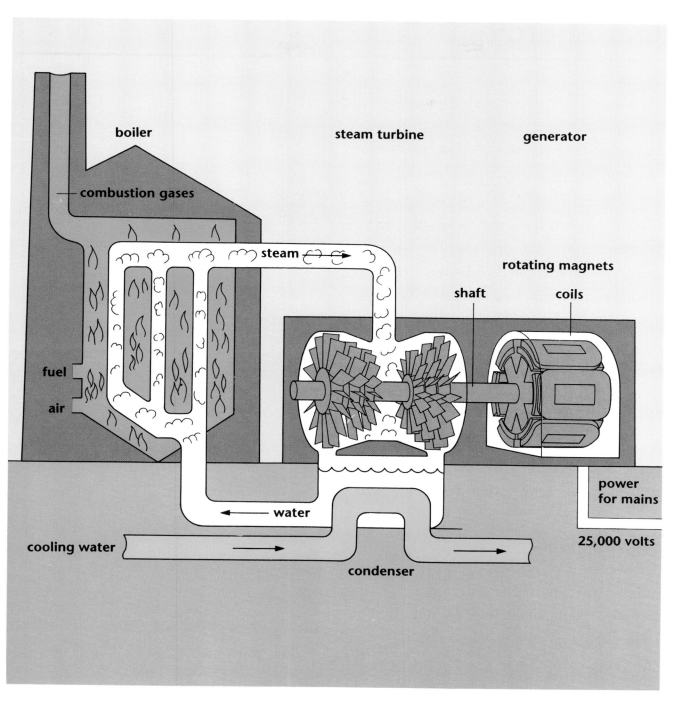

How a power station produces electricity

● **Focus**   fuel   turbine   generator   cooling tower

Nuclear energy

Everything in the universe, including the cells of your own body, is made up of billions of tiny particles. Every one of these particles has a **nucleus** or centre, which is a cluster of even smaller particles.

Usually the particles of the nucleus are held together tightly. But some kinds of materials have particles that can be split apart. This process is called **nuclear fission**. When this happens a great deal of **heat energy** is released. These kinds of materials are called **radioactive** materials.

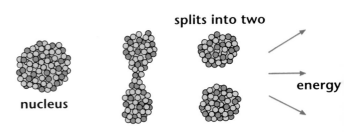

What happens when a particle splits

Nuclear power stations

A nuclear power station makes use of the energy in these radioactive materials. There are about 400 nuclear power stations around the world. They supply nearly one-fifth of the world's electricity.

Many nuclear power stations use the radioactive material called uranium. Uranium is a metal obtained from rocks. Uranium is a much more concentrated energy source than coal, oil, or gas. This means that a little uranium can produce a great deal of energy in the form of heat. The heat is used to boil water. The resulting steam pushes round turbines and these turn the generators that produce electricity.

A nuclear power station

 Electricity produced by nuclear power stations is exactly the same as electricity produced by fossil-fuelled power stations.

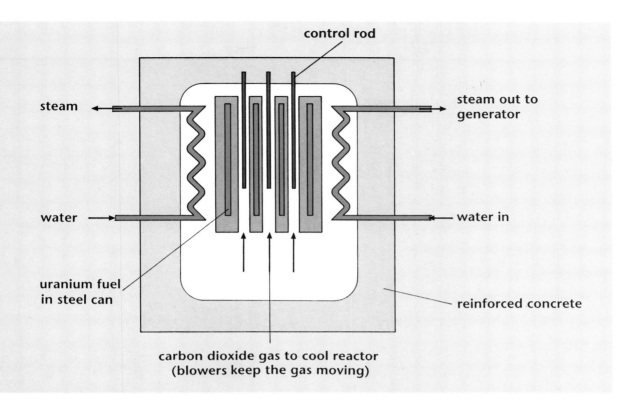

The nuclear reactor is the part of a nuclear power station where uranium is used to produce heat energy.

Dangers of nuclear energy

The process of splitting particles of uranium is very dangerous. So much heat is produced that there can be an explosion. The heat has to be taken away from the fuel quickly, before it can build up. It is taken from the fuel to the boilers by a stream of gas, or liquid metal, or water.

Radioactive materials give off a lot of dangerous rays called **radiations** that can harm, or even kill, people and other living things. The waste materials produced in a nuclear power station are also very radioactive and have to be disposed of with great care.

 Some radiations can pass through several metres of concrete.

Focus   nucleus   nuclear fission   heat energy   radioactive   radiation

Generating electricity without fuel

Using coal, oil or gas is not the only way of generating electricity. Supplies of these fuels will not last for ever. In addition, burning these fuels can cause pollution. Nuclear power stations can also cause dangerous pollution if radioactive material accidentally leaks out.

There are other ways of generating electricity using the energy of the Sun. These ways of generating electricity will not run out. They are **renewable**.

Wave, tidal, and solar energy

In a few places there are **wave power** stations that use the waves of the sea to drive their generators. There are also a few **tidal power** stations, with turbines, that are worked by the tides going in and out. Solar power stations change sunlight into electricity. Usually they use **solar cells** like the ones on solar-powered calculators. **Solar panels** use the heat from the Sun to provide heating.

This power station uses the Sun's energy to produce electricity.

Energy from hot rocks

In countries such as Iceland, Italy, New Zealand, and the USA there are **hot rocks** not far from the surface of the Earth. Sometimes there are hot springs, which shoot steam or hot water into the air. In some of these places, the steam or hot water is used to drive generators to produce electricity. In some places the hot water is used directly in central heating systems.

This power station uses heat from deep inside the Earth to help produce electricity.

Wind energy

The energy of the wind is enormous. In recent times new types of tall, slim **wind turbines** have been developed. Their blades can be 20 m long and they drive generators that make electricity.

A wind farm

Hydro-electric energy

Electricity can be made by using running water to spin turbines. These turn generators that make electricity. This kind of power station is called a **hydro-electric power** station ('hydro-' means 'water'). They are often built inside dams.

A hydro-electric power station

● Focus

renewable

wave power

tidal power

solar cell

solar panel

hot rocks

wind turbine

hydro-electric power

● **The earliest water wheels, which were really water turbines, were invented by the Greeks in about 100 BC.**

Getting electricity to the home

Electricity is carried from the power station to towns and villages by a network of wires. These make up what is called the **National Grid.** This carries electricity over the whole country.

🍎 **Birds sitting on electric wires are not harmed. The electricity does not pass into the birds' bodies because their feet are touching two places that are at the *same* voltage. Electricity flows only if there is a *difference* in voltage.**

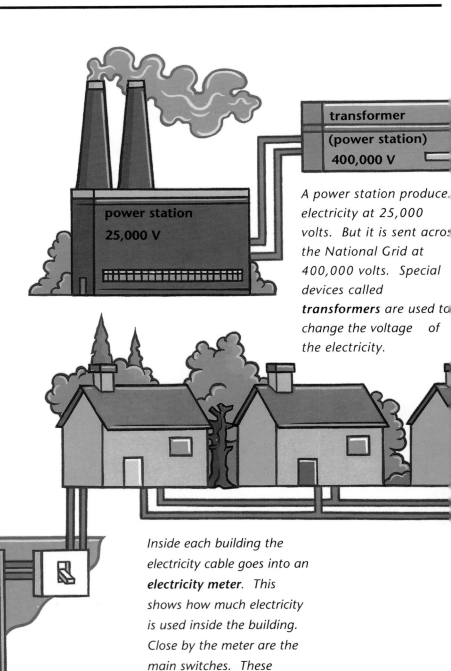

transformer

(power station)

400,000 V

power station

25,000 V

A power station produces electricity at 25,000 volts. But it is sent across the National Grid at 400,000 volts. Special devices called transformers are used to change the voltage of the electricity.

240 V

Inside each building the electricity cable goes into an electricity meter. This shows how much electricity is used inside the building. Close by the meter are the main switches. These switches can be used to turn the electricity off if something goes wrong.

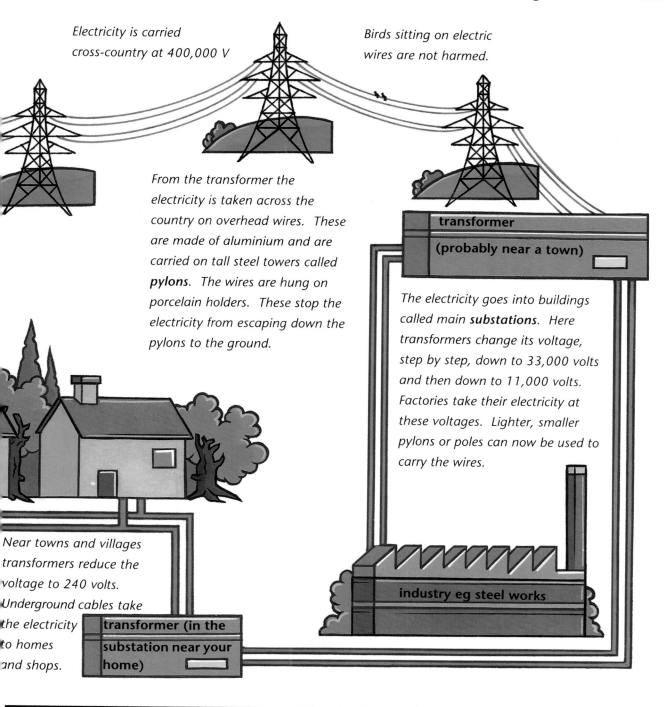

Only 80 volts is enough to kill an adult.

Electricity is carried cross-country at 400,000 V

Birds sitting on electric wires are not harmed.

*From the transformer the electricity is taken across the country on overhead wires. These are made of aluminium and are carried on tall steel towers called **pylons**. The wires are hung on porcelain holders. These stop the electricity from escaping down the pylons to the ground.*

transformer

(probably near a town)

*The electricity goes into buildings called main **substations**. Here transformers change its voltage, step by step, down to 33,000 volts and then down to 11,000 volts. Factories take their electricity at these voltages. Lighter, smaller pylons or poles can now be used to carry the wires.*

industry eg steel works

Near towns and villages transformers reduce the voltage to 240 volts. Underground cables take the electricity to homes and shops.

transformer (in the substation near your home)

Focus   National Grid   transformer   pylon   substation   electricity meter

Conductors, insulators, and short circuits

Conductors

Some materials let electricity flow through them. The aluminium wires on a pylon do this. Such materials are called **conductors**. Other metals such as iron and copper, are good conductors. So is the non-metal graphite, which is used in pencil 'leads'.

Many materials stop electricity passing through them. The porcelain discs on a pylon stop the electric current from going from the wires, into the pylon and down to the ground. Materials that stop electricity are called **insulators**.

Electricity pylons with insulators

Insulators

Engineers use insulators to stop electricity leaking into places where they do not want it to be or where it could do harm. A lot of common materials are insulators. Rubber, wood, plastics, cloth, paper, and air are all insulators. Electricity does not pass through them easily

The wires carrying electricity to a television set are covered in plastic. This is to protect anyone who touches them. The plug and socket are also made of plastic.

Plastic coverings help to keep us safe

Insulators	Conductors
wood	all metals
plastic	graphite
glass	you
dry air	damp air
paper	water
ceramics	anything wet
brick	
rubber	

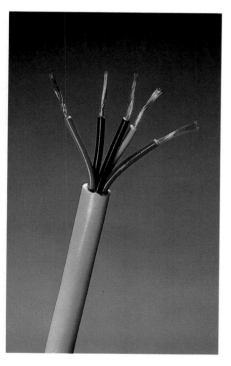

If the plastic insulation melts the wires will short-circuit.

Short circuits

Sometimes an electrical 'wire' is really lots of wires bundled together to form a **cable**. The wires cross over each other. If the wires were bare and they touched, electricity would cross from one wire to another. The electricity would not go where it was needed. When wires touch like this, it is called a **short circuit**. To prevent a short circuit, the wires are covered with an insulator such as rubber or plastic.

A short circuit can make wires get hot very quickly. They can start a fire in anything touching them. Many fires in buildings are started because the insulation on electrical cables is worn or broken, so that short circuits happen.

Air is an insulator most of the time. But if a voltage becomes very large, electricity can jump across air. Then you see a spark. Lightning is the spark created when a high voltage builds up between clouds and the ground.

Focus   conductor   insulator   cable   short circuit.

Electric lights

A wire made of a conductor lets electricity flow through it. But how much electricity can flow depends on how long the wire is, and what it is made of. The thinner the wire, the less electricity can flow. The longer the wire is, the less electricity can flow. More current will flow through a copper wire than through an iron one of the same size.

The amount by which a wire or any other object cuts down the electricity flowing through it is called its **resistance**. A long thin wire has a higher resistance than a short thick one of the same material. Wires made of insulating materials have the highest resistance. Those made from conductors have the lowest resistance. Even conducting materials have *some* resistance.

Light bulbs

Whenever electricity flows, it heats up the material it flows through. Inside a bulb is a very thin coiled wire, called a **filament**. When electricity goes through the filament, the thin wire becomes very hot. It gets so hot that it glows. The glowing filament gives our light. The bulb is filled with a special gas that stops the thin filament from burning away too quickly. A torch bulb works in the same way.

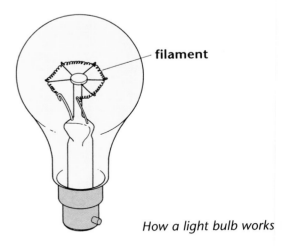

filament

How a light bulb works

 The electric light bulb was invented in 1879 by an American called Thomas Edison. His first bulb used a piece of scorched thread as a filament.

36

Fluorescent tubes

Fluorescent tubes are more often used in shops, offices, and factories than in homes. They work in quite a different way from an ordinary light bulb. The tube is filled with a gas called mercury vapour (mercury is the silvery metal found in some thermometers). When electricity passes through the tube, the mercury vapour gives a type of light called ultraviolet light. Ultraviolet light is invisible. But the inside of the tube is coated with a special kind of paint. When the ultraviolet light strikes this, the paint glows, giving off a bright light.

Some modern light bulbs, which use less electricity ('low-energy' bulbs), have a small coiled tube inside them.

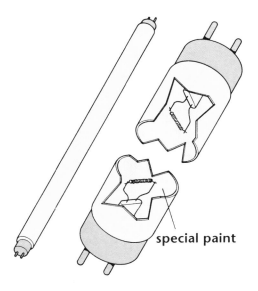

special paint

How a fluorescent tube works

Fluorescent tubes give an even light in large rooms.

Focus   resistance   filament   fluorescent tube

Fires and fuses

Electric heating

The main part of an electric fire is just a long piece of thin wire. The wire is made of a metal called nichrome, and it has a high **resistance**. It is wound round a rod made of an **insulator** such as fireclay. Fireclay can be heated to very high temperatures without bending or breaking. When electricity flows through the wire, the wire gets very hot. It glows and gives out heat. The wire used in the cable leading to the electric fire is made of thick copper. It has a much lower resistance to electricity and does not get hot.

Electric cookers, hair-driers, irons, and electric kettles all have **heating elements** similar to those in an electric fire.

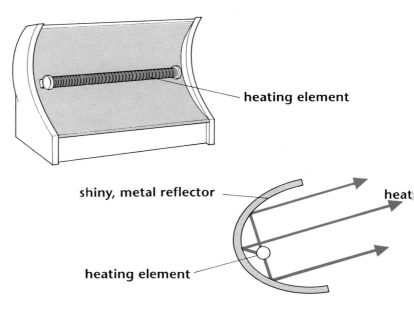

How an electric fire works

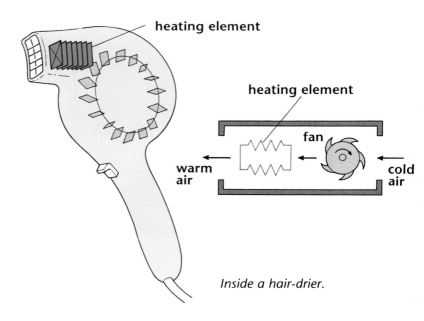

Inside a hair-drier.

Fuses

The heat given out by an electric current can be very useful. But it can also be very dangerous. If there is a fault in an electric circuit, or if an accident occurs, too much electricity can flow through a wire or cable. It can start a fire. Delicate electrical machines can also be damaged. To stop these things happening, there are **fuses** near the meter, where electric cables come into a building. There are also fuses in plugs and in machines connected to the mains.

A fuse is a thin wire with a low melting point. The fuse is part of the electrical circuit. If the right amount of electricity passes along the circuit, it can go through the fuse without difficulty. If too much electricity flows, the fuse heats up and quickly melts. It makes a gap in the circuit, which stops the electricity flowing.

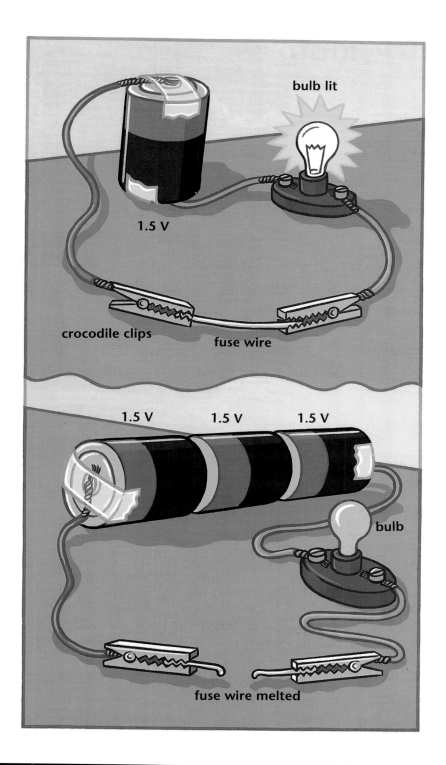

bulb lit

1.5 V

crocodile clips

fuse wire

1.5 V   1.5 V   1.5 V

bulb

fuse wire melted

 Focus   resistance   insulator   heating element   fuse

Electric motors

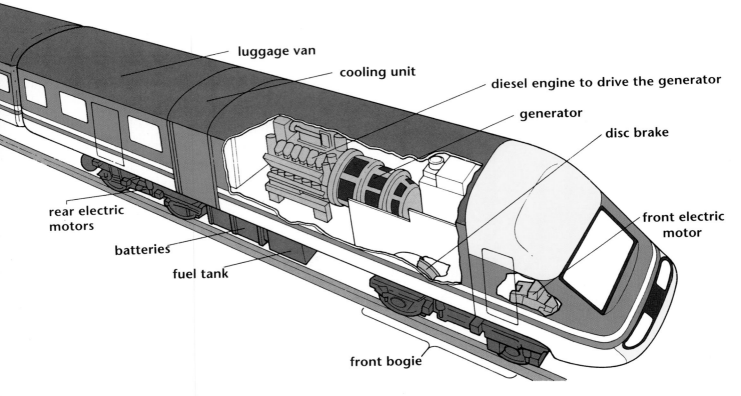

luggage van

cooling unit

diesel engine to drive the generator

generator

disc brake

rear electric motors

front electric motor

batteries

fuel tank

front bogie

An electric train uses large electric motors.

You see electric motors being used every day. There are electric motors in some toys and in many clocks and watches. Many household machines, including washing machines, dishwashers, vacuum cleaners, food-mixers and refrigerators have electric motors. Larger electric motors work lifts and electric trains.

An electric motor uses both electricity *and* magnetism. It contains a **coil of wire** and a bent **permanent magnet** on a spindle. When electricity flows through the coil, the coil becomes an electromagnet with **magnetic poles**. The north pole of the coil starts off near the north pole of the permanent magnet. The poles **repel** (push) each other, which makes the permanent magnet and the spindle rotate.

All these things use electric motors.

Focus   coil of wire   permanent magnet   magnetic pole   repel

Switches everywhere

A **switch** is a device that opens and closes a gap in a circuit – but switches do a lot more than just turning lights or machines on and off. Switches are important for controlling other things.

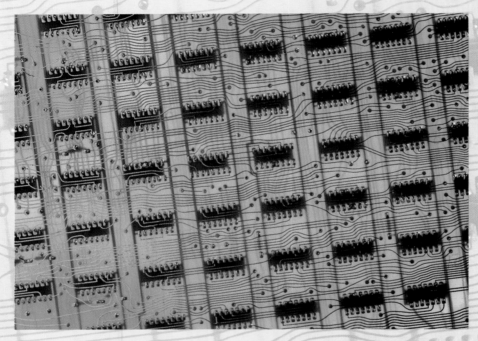

Inside a computer's microchips are possibly millions of tiny switches. They are too small to see. They are turned on and off by tiny electrical pulses called signals. The computer uses the switches to store data or information.

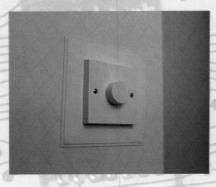

A dimmer switch

Dimmer switches

A dimmer switch varies the amount of electricity flowing through it. It can also stop the flow of electricity altogether. When the switch is turned to 'bright' a lot of electricity flows. If a bulb is in the circuit it glows brightly. When the switch is turned to 'dim' only a little electricity flows. A bulb would glow dimly.

Electric bells

In an electric bell an **electromagnet** switches the current on and off very rapidly. When the current is switched on, the electromagnet attracts a piece of iron attached to the arm of the bell's hammer. This pulls the hammer so that it strikes the bell. At the same time it stops the current flowing and switches off the electricity. The hammer is now pulled back by a spring. This process happens over and over again.

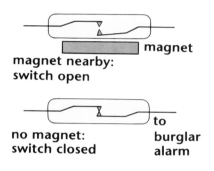

How an electric bell works

Burglar alarms

A burglar alarm switch is called a **sensor**. In one type a permanent magnet is fixed on a window or door. A special switch on the frame, contains an iron bar. When the window or door is closed, the magnet attracts the iron bar, keeping the switch open. If the window or door is opened, the magnet is moved. It no longer attracts the iron bar. A spring pulls the iron bar back so that it closes the switch. This lets current flow and makes the alarm ring.

A sensor switch helps to stop burglars.

Thermostats

Another common kind of switch is called a **thermostat**. It turns heaters or refrigerators on and off so that they stay at the right **temperature**. A thermostat contains a 'bimetallic' strip, which is really two strips, of different metals, joined together. The bimetallic strip bends when it is heated and straightens when it is cooled. As the strip bends it breaks the circuit and turns the electricity off. When the strip cools, it straightens, closing the circuit and turning the electricity on again.

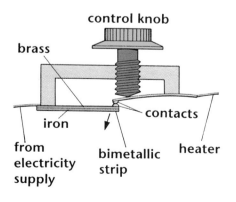

How a thermostat works

 Focus   switch   electromagnet   sensor   thermostat   temperature

Bright sparks

Electricity was known about long before people invented batteries and generators. In about 600 BC, the Greeks found that if a piece of amber was rubbed with cloth, it picked up small objects. Much later, in about AD 1570, an Englishman, William Gilbert, also experimented with amber. He called the effects he saw 'electricity', after the Greek word *elektron*, meaning amber.

The electricity from batteries and generators flows along wires and other conductors. It is called **current electricity**. The electricity made by rubbing amber is called **static electricity**, because it does not move.

Making static electricity

All static electricity is made when two objects or materials are rubbed together. Have you ever heard crackling sounds or seen little sparks when you undress? These sparks and crackles are caused by static electricity. The static electricity is made when certain materials, such as nylon, rub together.

If you rub a plastic comb on a woollen sleeve and then hold it over your dry hair, the hair may stand on end. This is because the comb has become **charged** with static electricity. Cling-film sticks to your hands because of static electricity.

Static electricity can make your hair stand on end!

Getting a shock

Static electricity can escape if it is given the chance to do so. Sometimes if you walk across a nylon carpet and then touch a door-handle, you get a small electric shock. Your shoes rub on the carpet and your body becomes charged with static electricity. When you touch the door handle the electricity escapes from your body into the door-handle, and you get a shock.

A lightning flash is caused by an electric force of about 100 million volts.

Lightning

Lightning is caused by static electricity building up in storm clouds. Rising air makes the tiny water droplets and particles of ice in the storm clouds rub together so that they become charged with static electricity. When enough static electric has built up, you see the electricity suddenly leap to another cloud or to the ground, as a flash of lightning.

A lightning-conductor is a thin strip of copper going from the top of a tall building to the ground. If lightning strikes the top of the building, the electricity will flow safely down the copper strip to the ground, instead of damaging the building.

Lightning may occur when static electricity builds up in the clouds.

Focus   current electricity   static electricity   charged

Rules to follow

Electricity is a great help to everyone. But it can also be dangerous. If you touch a bare wire from the mains, it can give you an electric shock, burn you and even kill you. Always follow these safety rules:

● **Never** overload a socket.

● **Never** connect wires to a socket without a plug.

● **Never** use an electrical device that has a worn cable.

● **Never** put electrical wires under a rug or carpet where they could be stretched or rubbed.

● Make sure the socket is switched off before plugging anything in.

● *Never* leave a television plugged in overnight.

● *Never* fly a kite or use a fishing rod near to overhead power cables. Even if your line does not touch the wires, electricity may jump the gap.

● *Never* plug an electric heater into a light socket.

Never touch electrical switches, ockets, or plugs with wet hands.

● *Never* touch or go too near to electric railway tracks, pylons or electricity substations. They can all be extremely dangerous.

Index

Note: the main reference for multiple entries is given in **bold** print.

Oxford University Press, Walton Street, Oxford OX2 6DP

*Oxford   New York   Toronto
Delhi   Bombay   Calcutta   Madras   Karachi
Kuala Lumpur   Singapore   Hong Kong   Tokyo
Nairobi   Dar es Salaam   Cape Town
Melbourne   Auckland   Madrid*
and associated companies in
Berlin   Ibadan

Oxford is a trademark of the Oxford University Press

© Terry Jennings 1994

First published 1994

ISBN   0 19 918333 3

A CIP record for this book is available from the British Library.

Acknowledgements

The publisher wishes to thank the following for supplying photographs:

AEA p 28; Boxmag Rapid p 12; Cull photographic pp 2, 6, 8, 10, 19 (bottom), 34 (bottom), 35, 42 (bottom), 44; Exide Batteries p 23; Peter Gould pp 3, 5, 22; Chris Honeywell pp 16, 17, 18, 19 (top), 20, 21; Dr T Jennings p 24 (bottom); Moorfields Eye Hospital p 13; National Grid Company plc p 34 (top); National Power p 25; Powergen p 26; Ann Ronan at Image Select p 24 (top); Shape Health Studios p 37; Sony UK p 11; Science Photo Library /Alex Bartel p 31 (top), /Tony Craddock p 42 (top), /Vaughan Fleming p 9, /Simon Frazer p 30 (bottom), /Keith Kent p 45, /John Mead p 31 (bottom), /Hank Morgan p 30 (top).

Cover photograph by Pictor International.

Mr Bean courtesy of Thames Television International.

The illustrations are by:

Jonathan Satchell and Oxford Illustrators.

Printed in France by Pollina, 85400 Luçon - n° 65428 - K